GO TO WWW.NOTGUDENUF.COM TO
HAVE FUN CREATING ILLUSTRATIONS
FEATURING YOU AND YOUR FRIENDS!

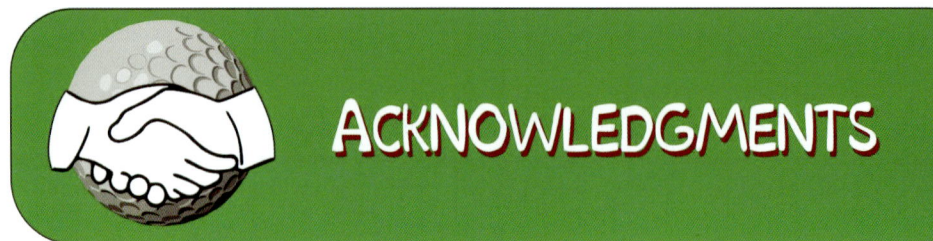

# ACKNOWLEDGMENTS

Bill Trantham, thanks so much for your insight and creativity in portraying each illustration.

Sam Esposito, on those days my ball has no zip code, I find solace in your inspirational advice that all is not lost if I dress impeccably to at least look the part.

My son, Jason, your computer savvy was invaluable, as I'd rather communicate with smoke signals.

My son, Todd, and "adopted" son, Aaron Webb, your rivalry validates that whether we're grinding for birdies or doubles, the influence of our psyche in the competition is universal!

My second "adopted" son, Evan Webb, many thanks for your printing counsel and services.

Aaron Schulman, your web design counsel was invaluable.

Tom, Deb, & Jake of Graphic Elite Printing, Inverness, Fl., your graphic designing was the final touch!

The best gurus in the business, Gravity Golf's David and Danny Lee, your insight into the swing mechanics has made the game more fun than ever.

The friendships of all who relieved a few bucks from the author or paid to see the show will never be forgotten.

MY FIRST AND BEST GOLFING COMPANION

ARTHUR "BUZZ" BUSBOOM

HIS UNWAVERING CHARACTER, RESPECTING HIS
COMPETITORS WITH BOTH CLASS AND DISARMING
HUMOR, BALANCING INTENSE COMPETITIVE STRENGTH
WITH A KIND AND GENTLE NATURE, SERVED TO ENDEAR
ALL WHO KNEW HIM, BOTH ON AND OFF THE LINKS

This book is affectionately dedicated to my Dad

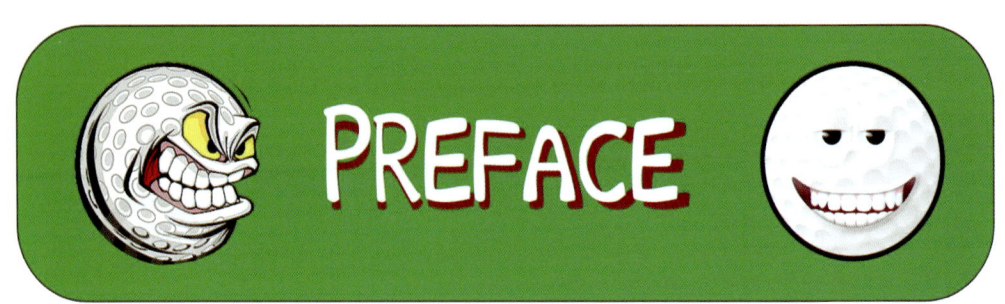

# PREFACE

After enduring the choice expletives of a struggling pro-am partner, Fuzzy Zoeller remarked, "You're not good enough to get mad!" His advice applies to every player, no matter what the caliber, from the week-end warrior playing for five bucks to the tour players who cut their teeth playing for the same five bucks. Invariably, the angrier you get, the worse you perform, not only on the links, but in virtually any challenge you may face.

When we first experience that symbiotic balance between body and mind, becoming one with the elements in that special round with Mr. Par at our side, logic is thrown to the wind, marking the beginning of a lifetime pursuit to relive that magical day. The journey is littered with missed shots challenging our body with the thought, "I know I'm better than this!", as we stare in disbelief at yet one more shot gone awry while muttering, "Where was my mind!"

One level of proof as to the extent of the game's ability to befuddle those who aspire to master it is to compare the number of golf publications and self-proclaimed gurus analyzing and offering instruction versus those in other sports. There are none even remotely close. When David Duval, at one time the world's #1 player, was asked what was the best tip given to him by his father, both an accomplished player and instructor himself, without hesitation he said, "Don't be afraid to go low," showing that not even the best of the best are immune from the demons. History is strewn with classic meltdowns of golf's greatest, like Duval, who never regained his former edge, or Norman's last round in the '96 Masters. The expression "early ripe, soon rotten" references this universal affliction as well, meaning if a player's first few holes are better than usual, he'll begin to question his ability to maintain that level of play, eventually returning to his comfort level as he finds himself staring at bad shots, especially down the stretch.

When you have a great round or pull off a really tough shot, savoring the feeling of accomplishment is much more satisfying if there's a few bucks on the line versus just having a "stroll in the park". When asked

ABOUT THE PRESSURE OF PLAYING ON THE PGA TOUR, LEE TREVINO REPLIED THAT IT DID NOT COMPARE TO WAGERING ON THE COURSE WITH NO MONEY IN HIS POCKET.

GAMBLING IN THE TRUEST SENSE OF THE WORD RELIES TOTALLY ON CHANCE, SO PLAYING FOR A FEW BUCKS ON THE GOLF COURSE ISN'T REALLY GAMBLING, SINCE IT INCORPORATES A MEASURE OF ONE'S ABILITY TO PERFORM UNDER PRESSURE, RESULTING IN A HIGHER COMFORT LEVEL WHEN COMPETING IN TOURNAMENT CONDITIONS. NOT ONLY DOES A PLAYER BECOME ACCUSTOMED TO PRESSURE, BUT HE'S ALSO MORE MOTIVATED TO PRACTICE, ENABLING HIS SHOT EXECUTION TO RELY MORE ON MUSCLE MEMORY AND HIS FOCUS TO BE STRATEGY AND VISUALIZATION INSTEAD OF THE MECHANICS OF THE SWING. THE EXPRESSION "THE DUMBER YOU ARE, THE BETTER YOU PLAY" MERELY POINTS OUT THE SIMPLER YOU CAN KEEP IT MENTALLY AND MECHANICALLY, THE BETTER YOU WILL PLAY.

AS IN ALL PROFESSIONAL SPORTS, THE CAREERS OF MOST TOUR PLAYERS ARE SHORT-LIVED, BUT THE TOUR'S UPPER ECHELON OF PLAYERS DOESN'T SEEM TO CHANGE MUCH EVEN THOUGH THEIR BALL STRIKING ABILITY IS BASICALLY THE SAME AS THAT OF THEIR FELLOW COMPETITORS. IT MUST BE CONCLUDED THAT THE TRULY GREAT PLAYERS HAVE AN INNATE MENTAL EDGE. THE ULTIMATE TESTIMONY REGARDING THIS INNATE ABILITY TO

CONSISTENTLY SCORE LOW UNDER PRESSURE IS THAT OF JACK NICKLAUS, REGARDED BY MANY AS THE GREATEST PLAYER IN HISTORY WITH 73 WINS INCLUDING 18 MAJORS. HE SAID FOR HIM THE FIRST THING TO GO WAS NOT HIS PHYSICAL ABILITY, BUT RATHER HE FOUND HIMSELF MAKING MORE MENTAL MISTAKES AS HE LOST SOME OF THAT INTENSE COMPETITIVE FOCUS THAT HAD CHARACTERIZED HIS PLAY THROUGHOUT HIS RECORD BREAKING CAREER.

IS THE RECORD OF ARNOLD PALMER ONE OF THE BEST IN THE HISTORY OF GOLF? ABSOLUTELY! IS THAT WHY HE IS REFERRED TO AS "THE KING"? NO. OF ALL THE LEGENDS TO PLAY THE GAME, HIS UNEQUALLED CHARISMA, COMBINING FUN AND APPROACHABILITY WITH COMPETITIVE INTENSITY, EPITOMIZES THE FACT THAT THE GAME OF GOLF IS JUST THAT, A GAME.

WHETHER YOU'RE A SCRATCH HANDICAP OR HAPPY TO BREAK 100, THE HOPE IS THE LIGHT-HEARTED PERSPECTIVE OF THIS ILLUSTRATED COLLECTION OF TIMELESS PORTRAYALS FAMILIAR TO VIRTUALLY ANYONE WHO PLAYS THE GAME, ALTHOUGH VOID OF TECHNICAL ADVICE, WILL HELP YOU APPROACH THE GAME WITH A SENSE OF HUMOR THAT WILL ELIMINATE THE DEMONS, SO YOU CAN FOCUS AND HAVE FUN AT THE SAME TIME, LOWERING YOUR SCORES AND ENRICHING NOT ONLY YOUR TIME ON THE LINKS BUT ALSO THAT OF YOUR FELLOW PLAYERS AND COMPETITORS.

# CONTENTS

WHEN IT COMES TO CONSIDERING HOW OUR PSYCHE AFFECTS US ON THE LINKS, NOBODY HAS MORE ON THE JOB TRAINING THAN THE CADDIES WHOSE JOB IS NOT ONLY TO PROVIDE COURSE KNOWLEDGE BUT ALSO TO BE BOTH A COUNSELOR AND A CONVENIENT EXCUSE FOR THEIR TROUBLED ARRAY OF CLIENTS. THE FOLLOWING PAGES DEPICT A FEW THOUGHTS THAT HAVE TO BE RACING THROUGH THEIR MINDS AS THEY BITE THEIR TONGUE WHILE LOOKING FORWARD TO THEIR FINAL CADDY DAYS WHEN IMPARTING THESE THOUGHTS TO THEIR SOON TO BE EX-EMPLOYERS IS NO LONGER A DISCRETIONARY CONCERN.

THE CLUBHOUSE STAFF, STOICALLY FACING THE SAME DILEMMA OF WHETHER OR NOT TO FOREGO DISCRETION, IS ACKNOWLEDGED IN THE FOLLOWING PAGES AS WELL.

3

LAST DAY?

APPROPRIATE RESPONSE?

OF ALL THOSE WHO RUIN THE FUN, ONE OF THE WORST OFFENDERS IS RABBIT EARS...

YOU'RE GETTING OLD WHEN NOBODY ASKS
YOU WHAT CLUB YOU HIT

FIVE HOUR ROUND

# TEACHER

IF YOU NEED TO LASER YOUR 2ND SHOT ON PAR 3'S, MAYBE IT'S TIME TO QUIT

# ZONER

THROW CLUBS FORWARD TO MAINTAIN
PACE OF PLAY

MOUTH

# TELECOMMUNICATOR

EXPLAINER

CLUB CHANGER

CHIRPER

TOKEN LOOK

**FISHERMAN**

## WHINER

# PRACTICER

## NEEDLER

**HUMAN RAIN DELAY**

NO ONE TAKES THE FUN OUT OF
PLAYING MORE THAN THE CHEATER.
A FRACTION OF 1% OF GOLFERS
WAGER ENOUGH TO MAKE IT A
LIFE-CHANGING ENDEAVOR, SO THE
DECISION TO COMMIT PETTY THEFT
AND RISK EMBARRASSING EXPOSURE
MUST BE DRIVEN BY A CONSCIENCE-
OVERRIDING EGO. ULTIMATELY, THE
CHEATER'S PLAY IS WORSE THAN IF
HONESTY HAD PREVAILED, SINCE AS
MUCH AS HE CHEATS HIS OPPONENT,
HE ENDS UP CHEATING HIS PEACE OF
MIND EXPONENTIALLY MORE.

# BASIC DROP

# DILEMMA

## FORWARD FUMBLE

# FOOT WEDGE

# BALL IN HAND IN SAND

THE FASTEST CART HAS THE BEST LIES

A STROKE DOES NOT OCCUR UNLESS SEEN

## GENEROUS DROP

## CLUB RATTLE

## FAKE MID-ROUND INJURY

IDENTIFYING THE BALL?

## DEAD BRANCH?

## CHEATING?

## PROVISIONAL BALL?

# HU$TLER NATIONAL GOLF CLUB

NASSAU, PRESS, AUTOMATICS, SKINS, CARRY-OVERS, MEDAL BET, WHIP OUT, CLOSE-OUTS, WOLF, HAMMER, BLIND DRAW, 9-POINT GAME, VEGAS, HIGH-LOW, QUOTA POINTS, GREENIES, SANDIES, PROXIES, ANIMALS

BEFORE STEPPING INTO THE GOLF WAGERING ARENA, FAMILIARIZING ONESELF WITH THE ABOVE TERMS WOULD BE A WISE DECISION. SOME OF THESE TERMS INVOLVE MULTIPLES THAT COULD CAUSE A SHORTFALL IN YOUR BUDGET. BASEBALL'S YOGI BERRA REFERENCED ONE OF THESE TERMS WITH ONE OF HIS CLASSIC EXPRESSIONS, "THE LESS YOU BET, THE MORE YOU LOSE, IF YOU WIN," WHEN HIS FRIENDS WON THE BACK NINE AFTER OPTING ON THE 10TH TEE TO FOREGO PRESSING THE BACK.

Beware of putting yourself in the "no money swing" situation, finding yourself thinking more about the money than the quality of the golf and ceasing to enjoy the competition. Play for enough to get your full attention, but not so much that your theme song is Kenny Rogers singing, "Don't count your money 'til the dealin's done."

A player should also be aware of the hustler, who sees himself as a "hired" entertainer, rationalizing his unwitting opponents are paying him to see the show. The best hustler is the one who chooses to only "rob from the rich to give to the poor". His opponents know going in their chances are slim at best and really consider the lopsided match as entertainment. Walking off the 18th green, he's not curtailed their lifestyle and has kept his annuity intact, leaving his opponents smiling and asking when they can play again, still believing there will be a different outcome next time. Combining this subtle salesmanship with skillful execution is truly an art and a sight to behold.

MOST HUSTLERS ARE PRETTY DARN GOOD PLAYERS, BUT YOU DON'T HAVE TO BE A GREAT PLAYER TO BE A GREAT HUSTLER. YOU JUST HAVE TO KNOW HOW GOOD YOU'RE NOT, NOT HOW GOOD YOU ARE. ONE OF THE BEST EXAMPLES WAS BOBBY RIGGS, A GREAT TENNIS STAR, BUT PROBABLY A 10 HANDICAP. WHAT A SHOW HE WOULD PUT ON! HE WAS THE ULTIMATE EXAMPLE OF "MOST BETS ARE WON OR LOST ON THE FIRST TEE" WITH HIS FAVORITE OXYMORON BEING, "I'VE CONSIDERED THE DISADVANTAGES OF A FAIR BET AND DECIDED THAT I NEED A FAIR ADVANTAGE." HE WOULD ALWAYS HAVE THE EDGE, RELYING MUCH OF THE TIME ON PLAYERS ACCEPTING BETS THEY KNEW WERE PROBABLY LOSING PROPOSITIONS BUT COULD SAY THEY LOST TO BOBBY RIGGS.

ALTHOUGH THE FOCUS ON THE FOLLOWING PAGES IS PLAYING FOR A FEW BUCKS ON THE LINKS, THE UNDERLYING THEME IS TO ENRICH THE EXPERIENCE FOR BOTH YOURSELF AND YOUR FELLOW COMPETITORS BY EMBRACING THE CHALLENGE OF EACH SHOT WITH HUMOR, MAKING THE COMPETITION A RELAXING AND FUN ESCAPE FROM LIFE'S REAL CHALLENGES.

# HU$TLER NATIONAL GOLF CLUB

## $$$$$ LOCAL RULES $$$$$

NO WHINING

NO GIMMEES

NO 14 CLUB RULE

NO IMPROVING LIES

NO PENCILS WITH ERASERS

NO SHOW PENALTY ... $100

NO EXTRA BALLS IN POCKETS

NO ADVISING OPPONENT PENALTY

NO BENDING OVER IN THE ROUGH

NO ANT OR BURROWING ANIMAL RELIEF

NO HANDICAP CHALLENGES ONCE PLAY BEGINS

NO BET CANCELLATIONS DUE TO INJURY OR WEATHER RELATED SUSPENSION OF PLAY...BETS PAID THROUGH COMPLETED HOLES

WALLET CHECK IN PRO SHOP BEFORE PLAY

10% BET MEDIATION OFFERED ... $100 MINIMUM

IT'S NOT REALLY LYING

YOU KNOW YOU'RE IN TROUBLE WHEN YOUR
OPPONENT HAS HIS HAND ON YOUR SHOULDER

## THE SET UP

# ARCH RIVALS

DEW SWEEPERS

68

MOST MATCHES ARE WON OR LOST
ON THE FIRST TEE

NO SHOW PENALTY

FIRST LIAR NEVER HAS A CHANCE

71

3 FRIENDS & A STRANGER

KEY TO WINNING...PICK THE RIGHT OPONENT

NO SYMPATHY

MEMORY LAPSE

SHAME 'EM INTO PLAYING

PLAYIN' THE GREEDY GO NEEDY CARD

THE OLDER I GET, THE BETTER I WAS

GETTIN' 'EM TO OVERTHINK

COURTESY LOOK

PROBABLY NOT IN THE USGA DECISIONS

TREES & SCREEN DOORS...90% AIR

JUST ANOTHER GREAT SHOT
RUINED BY A COMMENT

CAN YOU BELIEVE AS BAD AS WE'RE PLAYING WE'RE BEATING THESE GUYS!
YAH, OUR HAM AND EGG SHOW IS GETTING TO 'EM.
TRANTHAM 13

WE'LL PRESS YOU!
DROP YOUR SHOT ON 18 AND WE ACCEPT.
FORGET IT... YOU HAD YOUR CHANCE!
17 TEE
TRANTHAM 13

BACK NINE ADJUSTMENT

GETTIN' A SHOT

GIMMEE...AN AGREEMENT BETWEEN 2 PEOPLE WHO CAN'T PUTT

95

# FLAT-LINER

DANCIN' BUT CAN'T SEE THE BAND

## "LUCKY" HUSTLER

## EARLY CALL

NEVER MAKE A PUTT
YOU DON'T NEED TO MAKE

## SHAME 'EM INTO THE GIMMEE

IN THE DARK

CHUMMIN' THE WATERS

111

# THE CHOKE

YOU CAN CHOKE IN ANY SPORT, BUT MOST SPORTS ARE REACTION SPORTS WHERE YOU DON'T HAVE MUCH TIME TO THINK. BEFORE EACH SHOT A GOLFER HAS TIME TO THINK OF EVERYTHING FROM WHAT'S FOR DINNER TO WHY HE IS ON THIS EARTH. WITH EACH SUCCESSIVE SHOT THE GAME HAS BEEN KNOWN TO ESCALATE INTO AN INORDINATE EXTENSION OF THE SHOT MAKER'S BEING UNTIL HIS FRUSTRATION CONSUMES HIM WITH SEEMINGLY INSURMOUNTABLE ADVERSITY AND CONFUSION. IN ADDITION TO MASTERING THE PHYSICAL AND MENTAL INTRICACIES OF THE GAME SOME DEGREE OF GOOD FORTUNE COMES INTO PLAY AS WELL SINCE THE DESTINATIONS ARE A MERE $4\frac{1}{4}$ INCHES IN DIAMETER AT THE END OF PATHWAYS STRETCHING AS LONG AS 6 FOOTBALL FIELDS OVER, AROUND, AND THROUGH OBSTACLES AS CONTEMPTUOUS AS THEY ARE BEAUTIFUL.

THE IMPOSSIBILITY OF MASTERING ALL OF THESE VARIABLES, EVEN FOR TOP PROFESSIONALS, MAKES ADVERSITY MANAGEMENT AN INTEGRAL PART OF REACHING YOUR POTENTIAL WITH FUN BEING A KEY INGREDIENT. THE INTEGRITY, FORTITUDE, GRACE, AND SENSE OF HUMOR NEEDED TO MANAGE THE

ELEMENTS FACING PLAYERS ON ALMOST EVERY SHOT REVEAL PERSONALITY AND CHARACTER MORE THAN ANY INTERVIEW COULD EXPOSE, MAKING THE MOST IMPORTANT 6 INCHES IN GOLF BETWEEN THE EARS.

MOST CLUB CHAMPIONSHIP SCORES ARE HIGHER SINCE PLAYERS FEEL MORE PRESSURE THAN PROS WHO PLAY IN TOURNAMENTS EVERY WEEK, AND WE'VE ALL HIT THAT INFAMOUS BAD SHOT WHEN OUR NERVES GOT THE BETTER OF US PLAYING THROUGH ANOTHER GROUP...

## AUDIENCE CHOKE

A PLAYER CAN BE CRUISING ALONG AND ALLOW ONE BAD SHOT TO ESCALATE INTO A MELTDOWN RESULTING IN VISITS TO BOB ROTELLA ANALYZING WHY HE CAN'T FINISH OFF A GOOD ROUND AND GET IT TO THE BARN. LOWERING YOUR SCORING COMFORT ZONE AND AVOIDING THE "EARLY RIPE, SOON ROTTEN" SYNDROME MERELY INVOLVES NOT MAKING THE GAME BIGGER THAN IT IS BY JUST PLAYING ONE SHOT AT A TIME AND NOT CARRYING THE ADVERSITY OF YOUR PREVIOUS SHOTS INTO THE MINDSET OF THE NEXT.

THE OPERATIVE WORD IS "GAME", WHICH IMPLIES HAVING FUN. THE BEST QUARTERBACKS ARE NOT ONLY PHYSICALLY GREAT, BUT ALSO IMPART SUCH POSITIVE VIBES THAT EACH PLAYER LEAVES THE HUDDLE FOCUSED AND THINKING THAT NOBODY IS HAVING MORE FUN THAN ME! NO MATTER WHAT YOU DO, YOU'LL USUALLY DO IT BETTER WHEN YOU'RE HAVING FUN. PHIL MICHELSON STARTED WINNING MAJORS WHEN HE TOOK ADVICE TO SIMPLY SMILE, NO MATTER WHAT THE SITUATION. TRY IT. YOU'LL FIND THE MERE ACT OF SMILING WILL DRAIN THE TENSION FROM YOUR BODY, SO DON'T ALLOW A FEW BAD SHOTS TO RUIN YOUR DAY. YOU'RE NOT A BIONIC ROBOT. IT'S NOT HOW GOOD YOU HIT IT. IT'S HOW GOOD YOU MISS IT. EVEN THE BEST ONLY HIT ONE OR TWO "PERFECT" SHOTS IN 18 HOLES.

## PARALYSIS BY ANALYSIS

## CLUB CHAMPIONSHIP

## EARLY CHOKE

## GETTIN' FLIPPED

## NO MONEY SWING

RAINDANCE

IN THE LINE OF FIRE!

THERE'S NO MONEY IN COUNTIN' CHICKENS

## MONGOLIAN REVERSAL

WHEN YOU'RE ROOTING AGAINST YOUR
OPPONENT, YOU'RE IN TROUBLE

## BEGGAR

# DESPERATION

# IF YOU WANT IT BAD,
# YOU USUALLY GET IT BAD!

SPACIN' OUT

PRE-MELTDOWN GO TO SHOT...
THE FADE AWAY SKY HOOK

MID-ROUND WALK OFF

MELTDOWN!

# TRUNK-SLAMMER

## FIRST & LAST LESSON

# NOVICE

# TIME-SAVER

DIVORCE OPEN

# JUST REMEMBER...

WHEN YOU'RE HAVING FUN, YOU'LL PLAY BETTER AND ENRICH THOSE AROUND YOU, SO REALIZE THE LADIES ARE ALSO JUST TRYING TO HAVE A GOOD TIME. DON'T BE A FUN KILLER LIKE THE DIVORCE OPEN GUY WHO'S DECIDED NOT TO BE HAPPY BEFORE HE TEES OFF! EVEN IF SHE'S STRUGGLING, YOU CAN BOTH HAVE A GREAT DAY. JUST BE ENCOURAGING AND PATIENT AND VALUE YOUR TIME ON THE LINKS AS HAVING FUN TOGETHER, NOT OBLIGATORY SUFFERING. IF YOU CAN HAVE FUN ENCOURAGING OTHERS WHILE FOCUSING ON YOUR GAME AT THE SAME TIME, THE CALIBER OF YOUR GAME WILL IMPROVE AS YOU BECOME ACCUSTOMED TO PLAYING WITH DISTRACTIONS. THIS IS NOT TO SAY THE SHOE CAN'T BE ON THE OTHER FOOT WITH HER GIVING YOU SHOTS...NOT TO MENTION THE DAY WILL COME, IF NOT ALREADY, WHEN YOU WILL BE A SENIOR, LOOKING FOR A LITTLE ENCOURAGEMENT AND EMPATHY YOURSELF!

FRIENDSHIPS RESUME AND THE WINNER BUYS
AMIDST EXAGGERATIONS & LIES

MATCHIN' CARDS

# SANDBAGGER

THE LOSER IS ALWAYS INVITED BACK

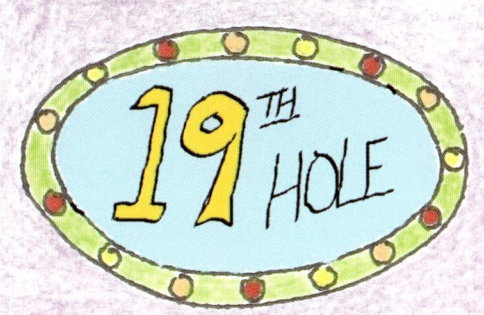

168

# WISDOM

# REMEMBERING AN OLD FRIEND...

I met Bobby Riggs after he and Billy Jean King gave a tennis exhibition at the Boca Grove Country Club. Less than an hour later, after representing my handicap as a 7, I found myself teeing it up for a hundred dollar Nassau. Since I was the first liar, he'd finagled 11 shots out of me, so even though I was 3-under standing on the 18th tee, I was out $200 and 1 down for another $200. Knowing it wasn't a stroke hole, I gave him a 1-down $200 press. He accepted only after I conceded to give him a half shot. I made par. Standing over a tricky 3-footer for par, he straightened up and said, "Boomer, if you give me this putt, I'll chalk off that $200 press!" I thought for a moment, knowing that would mean a $400 loss. If he made it, I'd lose $600, but if he missed, I'd break even. Thinking he would not be making that proposal if he was confident, I took a deep breath and replied, "I'll pay to see the show!" He didn't even hit the hole! *Pointing out that he was old enough to be my father, he then proposed a race to the cart for 50 bucks and let me say "Go!" I lost...wasn't even close! Embarrassing!*

Although best known for his loss to Billy Jean in the battle of the sexes, most people don't know that in 1939 he walked out of a British betting parlor with only $5 left in his pocket after wagering on himself to win the Wimbleton singles, doubles, and mixed doubles and then proceeded to win all three! He passed away in '95...sure miss him. He epitomized keeping the competition fun for everyone.

## *IF YOU THINK YOU CAN'T LOSE, YOU'LL LIKELY BE THE LOSER*

173

# CHARLIE

Since Charlie was a rather well-off annuity, his golf compatriots overlooked his lack of integrity and propensity for larceny on and off the golf course. Thinking nobody had a clue as to his antics, Charlie had some entertainment value as well. On one occasion the pro pulled aside one of Charlie's buddies, informing him Charlie had just stolen a golf glove. Considering it a "cost of doing business", his buddy told the pro just to put it on his bill. On another occasion Charlie was looking at a new lob wedge before going out to play. When Charlie pulled around to the bag drop after playing, the pro was standing there and told Charlie he couldn't find the wedge. As he directed the bag attendant to put his clubs on the back seat instead of in the trunk where he always stored them, Charlie replied the last he saw it was when he placed it back in the rack.

The best Charlie memory occurred at a charity event where each entrant picked up their tee gift of a dozen balls at the check-in area. One of his buddies observed Charlie slipping away with 5 dozen balls and stuffing them into his bag. A few minutes later his buddy took the 5 dozen balls out of Charlie's bag and returned them. After discovering on the first tee the balls were gone, facing the dilemma of being unable to share his trauma, Charlie shot a thousand.

## YOU LEARN A LOT ABOUT PEOPLE ON THE GOLF COURSE

# PLAYIN' BY THE RULES

TWO GOOD FRIENDS, AFTER BEING RAINED OUT AND HAVING A FEW BEVERAGES AT THE 19TH HOLE, NOTICED THE WEATHER HAD CLEARED AND CHALLENGED EACH OTHER TO A MATCH WHERE THE ONLY RULE WAS YOU CANNOT TOUCH YOUR BALL. ONE OF THE PLAYERS, AFTER HITTING HIS SHOT RIGHT DOWN THE MIDDLE, DISCOVERED HIS BALL COMPLETELY PLUGGED IN THE WET FAIRWAY. HE LOST THE HOLE WHEN THEIR AGREEMENT, "YOU CAN'T TOUCH YOUR BALL," WAS INVOKED BY HIS FELLOW COMPETITOR.

THE SAME UNFORTUNATE PLAYER HAD MORE BAD LUCK ON THE FOLLOWING HOLE, WHEN HIS TEE SHOT CAME TO REST ON A CART PATH. AFTER SEVERAL PRACTICE SWINGS, SCRAPING HIS IRON ON THE CART PATH, HE HIT A GREAT SHOT ON THE GREEN. HIS FRIEND REMARKED IN AMAZEMENT, "WOW! WHAT CLUB DID YOU HIT?" HE REPLIED, "YOUR 8-IRON."

## KNOW THE RULES! THEY CAN HELP YOU AS MUCH AS HURT YOU!

# AN OLD HUSTLER'S LAMENT

MY DREAM WAS ALWAYS TO COMPETE ON THE LINKS WITH THE VERY BEST. TO SAY PURSUING THIS GOAL CONSUMED ME WOULD BE AN UNDERSTATEMENT. THE HOURS, DAYS, MONTHS, AND YEARS I DEVOTED TO ACHIEVING THIS RECOGNITION PRETTY MUCH DEFINED ME. I KNEW IN MY HEART THERE WAS NO CHANCE OF ACTUALLY LIVING THE DREAM, EVEN ON AN AMATEUR LEVEL, LET ALONE AS A PROFESSIONAL.

I NURTURED BOTH MY EGO AND MY WALLET, PLAYING IN SERIOUS MONEY GAMES, ONLY IF I KNEW I HAD AN EDGE, NEARLY ALWAYS COVERING THE DRINKS AFTER SAVORING THE ACCOLADES AND DOLLARS COMING MY WAY. MY CLUB CHAMPIONSHIPS FELT LIKE U.S. OPEN VICTORIES TO ME, BUT I CAN'T RECALL MUCH ABOUT THEM, EXCEPT THE GENERAL CRITERIA WAS TO SIMPLY BREATH IN AND BREATH OUT FOR 18 HOLES.

OH, THERE WERE ALSO THOSE DAYS THAT I WOULD BLOW A CRUCIAL SHOT DOWN THE STRETCH OR MISS AN EASY PUTT TO GO FROM WINNING TO LOSING. MY LIFE SEEMED ALMOST MEANINGLESS ON THOSE OCCASIONS. WHEN I ARRIVED HOME, MY WIFE COULD SEE THAT I HAD LOST, AS MUCH AS I TRIED TO HIDE IT. ON THOSE NIGHTS I WOULD LIE THERE QUIETLY, RATIONALIZING THAT MY GOLF WAS A VALID PURSUIT AND A PROPER USE OF MY TALENTS, EVEN THOUGH I KNEW DOWN DEEP I WAS KIDDING MYSELF.

I RARELY, IF EVER, WOULD BE THE ONE TO PUT THE GAME TOGETHER BUT WAS NEVER WITHOUT ONE, AS THERE WERE DAILY INVITATIONS TO DO BATTLE, NONE OF WHICH DID I TURN DOWN. EVERYTHING TOOK A BACK SEAT TO THE ACTION ON THE LINKS. I COULD NOT LET GO OF THE HIGH OF WINNING, NO MATTER HOW TRIVIAL IT WAS, REFUSING TO ACCEPT THAT MY LIFE WAS ONE-DIMENSIONAL AND HAD NO BALANCE.

NOW THAT MY BODY IS BROKEN DOWN AND ALL MY GOLF COMPATRIOTS ARE GONE, I WISH I'D PLAYED MORE GOLF WITH MY KIDS. THEY'RE ALL HUNDREDS OF MILES AWAY, SO I DON'T SEE THEM MUCH. MY OLD FRIENDS WOULD BE FLABBERGASTED THAT I WISH MY WIFE AND I HAD PLAYED MORE GOLF AS WELL.

DON'T GET ME WRONG, I HAVE GREAT MEMORIES OF MY BATTLES ON THE LINKS, BUT ON MY LAST DAY I'LL BE THINKING ABOUT 3 THINGS...GOD, FAMILY, AND FRIENDS...IN THAT ORDER. THE GAME WOULD'VE BEEN A LOT MORE FUN IF I HAD THE WISDOM TO CONSIDER THAT THOUGHT EVERY DAY. I WISH MY VICTORIES COULD BE TRADED FOR MEMORIES OF APPRECIATING AND ENCOURAGING MY WIFE AND KIDS, MY FRIENDS, AND THOSE I'VE PLAYED BUT HAVE LONG FORGOTTEN, ENRICHING THEIR LIVES AS WELL AS MY OWN...MEMORIES THAT NOW I WILL NEVER HAVE.

NO OTHER GAME OFFERS THE CHANCE FOR GENUINE FELLOWSHIP IN A SETTING OF SUCH NATURAL BEAUTY AS MUCH AS GOLF, SO ENJOY YOUR TIME ON THE LINKS WITH THE PERSPECTIVE OF AN OLD HUSTLER.

## PERSPECTIVE

IN APPRECIATION OF YOU PARTING WITH YOUR HARD-EARNED CASH, THE AUTHOR WOULD LIKE TO SHARE SOME CHALLENGES YOU'LL WIN NEARLY EVERY TIME. JUST REMEMBER THAT BRINGING A CHUCKLE TO ALL IS WHAT'S MOST IMPORTANT WITH THE MONETARY CONSIDERATION, IF ANY, NEVER BEING SO GREAT AS TO DETRACT FROM THE COMPETITION BEING FUN FOR EVERYONE, WIN OR LOSE...

If your advantage over a prospective opponent is at least 18 shots, just say, "Let's have a close-out match. I'll give you 2 shots on #1, and if you're down coming into any hole, I'll give you 2 shots on that hole." The game can easily be manipulated to where the match is even coming into #18, so your advantage will be huge, yet you will only win one up.

When you have a long putt or chip, *casually* say, "You know, I think I can make this. I've got a $10 bill that says I can make it. If I can *show* you, you owe me $10. If I can't, I owe you $10. You should give me odds, but I'll do it even up." If you miss the putt, reach in your wallet, as if intending to pay, but instead show a $10 bill on which you've written, "I can make it." If you make it, just collect and say nothing as they stand there dumbfounded. Obviously, this can be done with a bill of any denomination.

Challenge a scratch player, especially one that's full of himself, that he can't break 80 if he hits 2 shots on every shot and has to hit the worst one on each successive pair of shots. For instance, on a par 4 he hits 2 tee shots, one in the fairway and the other slightly right. From the slightly right position he flags one shot with the other ending up on the edge of the green. From the edge of the green he chips one 2 feet from the hole and the other 6 feet. He now needs to make a 6-footer twice. Halfway into the round he'll be "fried" and begin to unravel like a cheap cigar.

IF YOUR HANDICAP IS AROUND 20, YOU'RE PROBABLY NOT ON MANY GREENS IN REGULATION, BUT YOU'RE PRETTY CLOSE, SO WHEN YOU MEET A SCRATCH PLAYER, JUST SAY, "YOU DON'T HAVE TO GIVE ME ANY SHOTS. JUST GIVE ME A FREE UNDER-HANDED TOSS ON EACH HOLE TO KEEP UP WITH YOUR DRIVE," BUT INSTEAD OF USING THE TOSS TO KEEP UP WITH HIS DRIVE, AS THE SCRATCH-HANDICAPPER ASSUMES, TAKE THE FREE TOSS WHEN YOU'RE NEAR THE GREEN. YOU'LL GET REALLY GOOD REALLY FAST AT THAT TOSS AND WILL HAVE SHORT PUTTS FOR BIRDIE ON JUST ABOUT EVERY HOLE, ALL BUT ASSURING YOUR SCORE TO BE IN THE 60'S.

PLACE A BALL ON THE FLOOR, A GREEN, OR TEE, CHOKE UP ON A PUTTER ABOUT 2 INCHES, TAKE A BACKSWING, AND BRING THE BUTT END OF THE GRIP DOWN TO THE BALL, TAPPING IT A FEW FEET. THE CHANCE OF YOU TAPPING THE BALL ON THE FIRST TRY IS REMOTE. MOST PEOPLE PULL ON THEIR DOWNSWING CAUSING TENSION IN THE ARM MUSCLES WHICH IN TURN GOES INTO THE CORE OF THE BODY. THIS TENSION MAKES IT VIRTUALLY IMPOSSIBLE TO GET DOWN TO THE BALL. PRACTICE BY TAKING THE TENSION TOTALLY OUT OF YOUR ARMS. AS YOU APPROACH THE BALL, SLIGHTLY OPEN YOUR FINGERS WHICH NOT ONLY TAKES MORE TENSION OUT OF YOUR ARMS BUT ALSO EXTENDS YOUR REACH. IT'S REALLY FUNNY WHEN AN OLDER PLAYER CAN DO IT AND AN UNWITTING YOUNGER PLAYER CANNOT. AFTER YOU DEMONSTRATE HOW EASY IT IS, CHALLENGE THEM TO DO IT ON THE *FIRST* TRY.

# ONE MORE THING BEFORE I GO...

I'D LIKE TO REFERENCE THE "FORMULA", A GLIMPSE INTO MY PERSPECTIVE WHEN CREATING THIS ADDITION TO THE LIBRARIES OF BOB ROTELLA AND HIS COLLEAGUES.

UNLIKE MOST SPORTS, DIFFERENT CALIBER GOLFERS CAN ENJOY THE FUN OF COMPETING AGAINST EACH OTHER, SO THE GAME HAS AFFORDED ME THE OPPORTUNITY TO MEET AND DEVELOP FRIENDSHIPS WITH PEOPLE OF ALL SKILL LEVELS FROM FIVE CONTINENTS AND ALL WALKS OF LIFE FROM THE AVERAGE JOE TO CEO'S AND CELEBRITIES. ON THE LINKS NOBODY CARES ABOUT THE OTHER'S STATION IN LIFE, AS THE COMMON BOND, THE FUN OF THE COMPETITION, IS THE FOCUS AND GREAT EQUALIZER, ERASING CONSIDERATIONS OF BACKGROUND AND ACCOMPLISHMENTS.

THAT BEING SAID, NOBODY LIKES TO LOSE. SHOW ME SOMEBODY WHO DOESN'T MIND LOSING, AND I'LL SHOW YOU A LOSER. SINCE HANDICAPS ARE BASED ON THE BEST 10 SCORES OUT OF THE LAST 20, PLAYERS WHO ARE INCONSISTENT WILL PLAY BAD HALF THE TIME AND LOSE. WHEN THEY SHOOT THEIR HANDICAP, THEY'LL WIN 50% OF THOSE ROUNDS, RESULTING IN A 75% LOSS RATIO, SO INSTEAD OF GETTING OR GIVING STROKES BASED ON HANDICAPS, DROP OR GIVE AN ADDITIONAL SHOT BASED ON THE WIN OR LOSS IN THE PREVIOUS ROUND. THAT WAY OVER A PERIOD OF TIME THE MONETARY EXCHANGE WILL BE RELATIVELY EVEN WITH NOBODY GETTING THE SHORT END OF THE STICK, ELIMINATING QUESTIONS ABOUT HANDICAPS WHILE KEEPING FRIENDSHIPS INTACT AND THE FUN IN THE GAME. AFTER ALL, THE PURPOSE OF PLAYING FOR A FEW BUCKS IS REALLY TO TEST YOUR PSYCHE WITH THE FOCUS ON THE TRANSFER OF THE MONEY, NOT THE AMOUNT.